MUDAS, AND HOME OFFICE.

By

Ricardo Alonso Rodriguez Rodriguez

Content

MUDAS

The MUDAS represent a lack of productivity within a business, whether it's an office or a manufacturing plant. They embody the absence of standardization, assigned activities, or the insufficient fine-tuning of the process. Businesses strive to understand what happens against inertia, which involves undertaking large projects while remedying problems without stopping. If you're familiar with MUDAS, you'll know that you halt activities to understand common problems, learn from them, and leave evidence. MUDAS are related to:

- **Lack of activity analysis**: This involves understanding what happens when a nut is assembled, writing a number 10 on a list, going through a shipping manifest while trying to match quantities and part numbers, and understanding the effort to move and assemble pieces. This analysis must be comprehensive because most people think first in terms of dollars in a thrift shop rather than a business. They don't see the transaction but a shirt with a dollar sign stitched to the fabric. This means that problems are often underestimated or not dealt with and are balanced out through monthly results.
- **Lack of workload analysis**: Workload can be balanced without analyzing the timing for each step of the process. Instead of identifying the reasons for fluctuations (model mix, unreliable tool, reworks), these are distributed among different resources, hiding the problem.
- **Perception of idleness**: Have you heard about the 36-hours marathon at the office? What if you get things done within your regular 9-5 job? One type of boss might think it's effective, but another might deem it slacking.

- **Lack of process or tools for analysis**: Decisions are often made subjectively instead of being based on information form the process or from a similar process.

For a house, you can improvise a desk stand using a tower of cereal boxes, o using the dining table as a work desk. But it is the same as a lack of design of spaces inside the house.

Today, you can identify MUDAS as having two cell phones – one for work and another for personal use – which increases attention and response to both devices and splits your productivity between realms.

Not having the ideal place for reading, studying, or even listening to soothing music can be a challenge. However, we've lived with these issues since time immemorial. Today, you might find yourself:

- Juggling two cell phones, one for work and another for personal use. This increases your attention and response to both devices, splitting your productivity. It's like wearing different hats depending on the phone you're using. However, it's not as simple as that because both phones are always on and ready. In this context, your work phone becomes an extension of your workspace, ready for virtual meetings or even to serve as a hotspot for your computer. Therefore, it's important to set up quiet hours on your phone.

- Accumulating pleasures in life like books and music without truly enjoying or reflecting on them. Hoarding is not the same as enjoyment. Having too many things often reflects possession rather than reflection. Adding desired items to your to-do list doesn't necessarily help develop a hobby or provide a meaningful end to a demanding day.

- Owning more than two cars out of vanity or for collection purposes. This requires movement, maintenance, and space to keep them safe from the elements. Greed doesn't equate to careful planning but rather having any resource ready at any time for any purpose.

Up to this point, a "muda" (waste) is anything that requires extra movement and resources to maintain, keep safe, turn on, or preserve. Some of these are hobbies and others are compartmentalization of one's attention. The difference may lie in discipline and planning:

- Cars require scheduling services based on mileage and budgeting to keep them running. Appreciating the story behind the car's design and sharing this admiration through appreciation groups or clubs is part of resilience.

- Phones require setting daily usage hours to address each issue appropriately and charging them somewhere apart from your bedroom in respect of your rest hours. Keeping them away from the dinner table prioritizes quality time with your family. This is also part of resilience.

- Music and books require understanding who wrote them, when they were written, and why they were written. This too is resilience.

"MUDAS" or wastes need to be understood from three different perspectives:

1. **Personal Resources**: These are resources that have meaning or help create a hobby, a business, or a lifestyle. They are related to who you are and why you exist. They provide meaning.

2. **Home Office**: Unlike traditional businesses, home offices require disciplined attention and decision-making. In Mexico, where the concept of home office is relatively new, it's important to maintain clear boundaries between work hours and personal time, as well as between home activities and business-related activities. Operations that need to happen at home, such as cleaning, kitchen duties, procurement, and legal obligations (like taxes), were often neglected because people were not traveling or commuting. However, they still need to happen. In a home office, "mudas" often manifest as piled-up obligations and analyses because you're engaged and not moving around. The user's productivity is paramount in a home office setting, not tools and fixtures like in a factory. Any hindrance to user productivity due to overproduction and overprocessing of data is considered a "muda".

3. **Factory**: In a factory setting, resources include tools, fixtures, raw materials, and operators. Their productivity is key. Having the right information and materials is essential for making the right decisions. A factory is a complex network of decisions that requires the right information in the

right amount at the right time in the right place. Any sacrifice due to intolerance to stress can lead to poor decisions. Business-oriented results are everything.

"MUDAS" should be translated into these perspectives to cover who you are, what you do at the office, and what the organization does:

- **Who You Are**: As mentioned before, resilience enables a person to deal with pressure through safety habits of work hours, exercise, reflection. It also gives a sense of how the person can deal with priorities first without avoiding tough items that can slow work down.

- **What You Do at Work**: Providing the proper space and mindset for dealing with items requiring full attention is crucial. This might be challenging in a home office setting where the same space might be shared with other family members or pets.

- **How Productive Are Operations**: Having resources invested in making the right goods in the right amount at the right moment in the right space is key. There should be no second thoughts about tools and fixtures; design defects should be dealt with before customer quotes.

Let's delve deeper into "MUDAS", which include Defects, Waiting, Overproduction, Overprocessing, Transport, Movement, and Inventory. These terms describe the effect of waste on operations; they are easy words used to catalogue, dispose of, and remove waste from operations.

These wastes primarily belong to manufacturing and stem from deficient engineering design, inadequate manufacturing cell and operations design, insufficient follow-up to production logs, and overprocessing owned by the company due to uncertain production conditions that could result in defects in the customer's product.

"MUDAS" occur on the production floor where the transformation process happens and delivers finished goods for the next link in the value stream. A defect can trigger all the other six wastes. Regardless of the situation, it will disrupt the production flow, test the controls to prevent more problems, and eventually one of them will fail. While wastes occur on the production floor, their origin lies at the management level. As mentioned earlier, wastes are embedded into the design due to mistakes made or a failure to focus on testing controls and carefully considering countermeasures to avoid further production issues.

Now, let's consider Home and Home Office (or office) environments. Their "MUDAS" or wastes should not be identical:

Defects are part of one's life at home and are a testament to character. It's not about the strength and resolution to overcome them. However, consider how they can perpetuate even further - a wall that some call reality, others sacrifice. The problem is never owned nor is there a will to name it.

OVERPRODUCTION

This waste occurs when material or product is created beyond the required amount. It consumes every resource into production without a specific requirement or request. For instance, imagine cooking for 10 people when it's only for yourself. The excess food will wither, lose flavor, and attract flies until someone eats it or it's thrown away. Similarly, consuming canned soda when you only need water leads to empty cans in the trash bin and excess sugar accumulating in your body. Both examples require energy to be created or consumed and occupy space, whether it's food in the pantry or cans in the trash bin.

In a manufacturing context, overproduction creates inventories and spends resources on creating needless items. Dusty products covered in trash are a perfect example of wasted resources. Overproduction satisfies only momentary needs like hunger or thirst.

In a Home Office or Home setting, discipline is required to avoid overproduction of information. For platforms like YouTube and Instagram, overproduction might seem like a means to expose content. However, it can also dilute the message and render the content pointless. Excessive emails on one topic due to lack of focus can bloat the inbox with useless information and overwhelm the reader. Overproduction of information is an enemy in home office settings, comparable to mindlessly scrolling through TV channels while lounging on your sofa.

The solution to overproduction is to focus on your goals and maintain a clear purpose. If only one person will eat, cook for one person. If you're creating content, have a clear idea of what you want to create and show. If you're in production, have the orders and amounts on hand so everyone has a clear idea of what needs to be done. Overproduction isn't about trying; it's about dealing with unnecessary items and waste.

Costs related to overproduction include:

- Building and maintaining large warehouses; keeping inventory lists updated, racks in good shape, and forklifts maintained.

- Installing and cleaning extra shelves; maintaining extra space waiting for a purpose.

- Hiring extra workers and machines to break down some of the bottleneck operations. This includes training, procuring gear, and building utility drops.

- Using extra containers for excess food; keeping them clean, stored, and arranged. While this might not make sense at home, it requires time in a space that could be used for other activities.

- Wasting time deleting extra emails due to subscriptions. Unneeded information absorbs time through managing subscriptions, discarding alerts, and potentially exposing your information to threats.

- Having extra parts and materials. This is like having an extra car for parts. It will sit in a corner, occupying productive space, leaking oil on the floor, while being consumed for other jobs or still having useful parts.

- Using extra energy, oil, electricity, and pneumatic air. Even if capacity is not an issue, overproduction can lead to requiring extra energy from utility droppings in the same shift but the utilization will not be paid for.

- Having extra forklifts, tow trucks, pallets, and skids to manage material across the production plant or warehouse.

- Hidden problems and invisible Kaizen points.

- Extra transactional costs like managing the bill of materials, issuing new production orders, keeping track of material through ERP.

- Extra and bigger clothes due to overweight (the fat overproduction by drinking lots of soft drinks).

Overproduction is a root cause of other types of waste or "muda":

- **Motion**: Workers are busy producing items that haven't been ordered. Their work isn't compensated by any sale, and their effort will also be needed to move and store the excess inventory.

- **Waiting**: This is often related to large batch sizes. Working with batches means finishing one batch before moving on to the next step in the process, which involves preparing to receive and process it. With proper coordination, there won't be any waiting for the overproduced pieces to complete the batch before being moved.

- **Conveyance**: Unnecessary finished goods must be moved to storage warehouses. In a home office setting, this could mean transmitting large-sized emails.

- **Correction**: Early detection of defects is more challenging with large batches. Defects are hidden in numbers, and it requires extra effort to find the root of the problem while managing excess items.

- **Inventory**: Overproduction leads to unnecessary raw materials, parts, and work-in-progress (WIP). These will need to be managed, moved, and stored. Also, raw materials have been used for items that won't be needed but are required for products that are in demand. Sometimes this will necessitate procuring extra raw materials, which if urgent, will be brought urgently to the facility and incur extra fees for the deviation in shipping and orders.

Overproduction means that resources are engaged in activities that won't translate into sold items, are not a priority, or are not related to their roles. It also involves producing items before a customer order is placed or generating unneeded information. Here are some examples of overproduction:

- **Processing Non-Priority Customer Orders**: This leaves priority orders out of shift or requires extra time. If ERP information is not completely reviewed, priority orders may not be checked for available raw material, or the queue time may not be enough to finish the order in time.

- **Processing/Inspecting Non-Priority Finished Goods**: This leaves priority orders last, requiring extra time if needed. You might finish these goods, but not in time for shipping, which could require extra time in shipping and delay truck long enough to compromise other production orders that were completed on time.

- **Creating a File Without Additional Information**: This can lead to information being left in a tray or inbox without any further information added, hidden until it is required and will need to be completed. If not dealt with correctly, it can stop a process while trying to correct the defects in its information.

- **Printing Extra Material for Customers and Coworkers**: This can lead to the management of sensitive, customer-owned information that will need to be managed if left unused, probably cancelled, or destroyed to avoid the spread of confidential information.

- **Creating Additional ID Tags for Personnel**: Resources are compromised on tags that will not be used. These can become an issue if these have the clearance to enter facilities, or material is short to make the proper onboarding for incoming new employees.

- **Creating Inventory Locations for Nonexistent Part Numbers**: Dealing with overproduction might require creating and managing these at the warehouse or raw material level, taking and putting them in the storage location assigned and making sure that the system can absorb the inventory in future production orders.

- **Running Out of Raw Material for Priority Customer Orders**: The production system already used the material critical for priority orders on overproduction. To avoid further modification to the goods, the company will seek to bring the raw material urgently, making an effort in placing urgent purchase orders, expediting shipment, and having it received out of business hours. All of this incurs an extra cost due to poorly reviewed information or systems that can allow this waste.

Shifting gears to overproduction in life, it's about managing your commitments without jeopardizing your relationships, financial stability, and cultural goals. The key is understanding that being present and having time are not the same because life happens and work has a schedule. Some companies tend to ignore this balance and demand more time than what's stipulated in contracts. Some even include a clause allowing an open time window if required by their supervisor.

A story that comes to mind involves the seats of a Mustang. The production setup was already behind schedule for the customer's start of production. To alleviate the plant manager's stress about not having a contingency plan in case of missing the customer's date, people were assigned to be present at the plant during the last week of 2019 and the first week of 2020. However, setting up a production line requires materials, tools, setup devices like cameras and torque tools, purchasing required items, updating standard work sheets, and having the right people to support these tasks.

The problem was that these weeks were holidays in Mexico, and no task could be advanced due to lack of support. This resulted in overproducing idle time due to poor planning and absence of the team, which can rob quality time with family. Not everyone is equipped to handle such stress.

Identify overproduction not by the amount of excess inventory on the production floor without a production order, but by following these steps:

1. Obtain a copy of the production floor layout. Identify all the workstations on the layout by name and number in the process sequence. Ensure the flow of materials and products is included in the drawing.

2. Update the layout with any unidentified workstations. Make these updates as quickly as possible so that notes taken on the process are related to interactions, not missing information.

3. Identify the production supervisor locations on the layout, or where the supervisor stands while the process is running. This can be understood by visiting the production floor and taking notes on the dynamics.

4. Note on the layout where production control, production plan, and hour-by-hour status are located. Understand who is responsible for sharing information about part numbers to manufacture with the production floor, or if it's a broadcast system that reacts only to customer orders and not manual programming. Determine if there's a possibility that the program can be modified and whether there's clarity and transparency about where requirements are coming from.

5. Understand how the information of the production plan is updated. Identify if there's a manual update, whether information goes along with the product, or if it's a kitting system that only supplies material required by the production order in exact quantity.

6. Look for nameplates and testers that identify the product by part number and serial number to trace product status through the process. Note if this information is entered manually or automatically and if there's a control step that notifies when a number is duplicated.

7. Check on the layout for critical operations in the process and look for countermeasure plans in case of a risk of shutdown due to a critical operation.

8. Check on the layout and physically for an evident flow in the process, which can help direct materials through operations without risk of mixing components.

Here are the revised notes from the assessment:

- The layout is not updated, or the process at production has not been followed to reflect the actual operation. This could mean that changes to operations, materials supplied, and equipment are not represented on the layout. This could also impact the flowchart and FMEA if there's no habit of updating documents, indicating that controls may not have been assessed for changes in operation.

- Manual modifications to the production plan can disrupt material flow or job sequences at workstations, leading to confusion about component availability. This disruption can require additional material and result in excess material at the workstation.

- The production plan is not diligently followed and tracked on a production system. The available system is an hour-by-hour board.

- The flow of materials through operations is not visible, or there are no logical visual steps. This could lead to materials being lost or not used where required.

- Critical operations are not identified, which could mean that there's no traceability of components processed at the station. There may also be no countermeasures in place in case of a breakdown.

- Nameplates and serials that are not identified as duplicated could pose a problem in tracing parts produced for test results. This could be an issue if traceability is a customer requirement.

OVERPROCESSING

Performing unnecessary steps, such as making a cake in the oven, fabricating a new fixture in the machine center, manufacturing parts for a finished good like a seat or a high voltage switch, or conducting a new assessment on warehouse capacity, can lead to waste. This is especially true if it takes more time to process due to poor tool and product design, making it difficult for the operator to access the assembly or locate the component.

Waste can also be generated from worn-out tools or fixtures due to excessive contact between parts or high torque values, machine downtime due to exceeded capacity, and producing defects that later have to be reworked. This could potentially deviate the process to fix the product and add steps different from those declared on standard work sheets or on the PFMEA.

Providing higher-quality products than what is required by the customer with a process that was poorly designed and probably underestimated on the cost sheet can also lead to waste.

Overprocessing can be avoided by doing everything right the first time, such as:

- Quoting a product with a carefully analyzed design and process.

- Reviewing the design before meeting with the client to ensure components are clearly oriented and located against each other to avoid assembly mistakes.

- Reviewing torque values and required materials so that available tools and equipment can meet the assembly rate and specifications.

- Reviewing the master data files, or files with basic information, to verify customer part numbers, component part numbers, consumption locations, lot size, and batch size declared in the ERP.

- Comparing the design against the master data files to review the required quantity per finished goods part numbers. This helps ensure every required part can be accounted for.

- Reviewing every bit of information in ERP to check the scrap percentage per part number and enable backflush, so that every finished good can account for or discount components from the system. This helps planners have accurate material availability information.

- Checking the information needed for your driver's license to avoid any further movement to get the required paperwork.

- Assessing the logistics operation to avoid being blindsided by savings from moving the manufacturing operation from one site to another.

- Gathering all necessary information to create a comprehensive report.

Regrettably, some steps are prerequisites to move the process forward, meaning you cannot proceed without them being completed or present. Circumstances may push teams to act without the right information, potentially carrying mistakes further into the project implementation. Addressing these mistakes will require time, resources, and capital; and in some cases, it may not be possible to rectify the problem.

Overprocessing is a particularly messy type of waste because it demands additional resources to manage and may require extra capital to change tooling or generate additional costs without any way to compensate at startup.

Attempting to add more value to a service or product than what your customers are willing to pay for is a result of a failed assessment, poorly conducted review of processes, or underestimated documents needed for formalities. However, knowing that customers will not pay for it, the company might choose to absorb the impact of overprocessing out of the profit margin.

Overprocessing can be understood as:

- Not knowing what your customers want and adding more value than they're willing to pay for. This often happens when everything is done according to the professionalism of a craftsperson.

- Not knowing what the process is, leading to additional tasks that the customer won't pay for and that will impact the financial health of the company.

- Allowing non-value-added work to creep into a process. This could be unplanned steps that require an extra resource to get or put a component, or assuming that it is required and will be done altogether. Someone will do it, and that's the problem because it's not part of the business case. The excuse often given is that the process sheet is a living document and will be modified throughout the project.

- The worst reason for overprocessing is fear of failure because there's still a reminiscence of a father figure in your boss. As a result, the evaluation and case study are done with figures and facts put together in a mediocre fashion.

Examples of overprocessing include:

- Adding a bag to your product for extra protection, even if the package already has cushioning. This is protection over protection or adding individual bubble wrap to each egg in an impact-resistant box.

- A work instruction requiring sign-off by several team members, then requiring approval by document control, and then requiring an electronic approval, having the physical document posted at the workstation to be signed by the approvers. This is a poorly designed procedure to get a physical copy into practice.

- Overengineering a problem when brainstorming might actually work as well and also result in reliable products for the customer. This is oversimplified but brainstorming through careful hypothesis might help understand the problem. Then, having a DOE performed to optimize the process.

- A FTQ without strategic focus. A KPI that only requires improvement without perspective or guidance on how to do so. In the end, it will require questioning the direction of this KPI so that it matches upper management requirements. And this will be related to a lack of management direction, micromanagement, or first-time managers.

- An A3 without cross-functional items or validated activities, put bluntly without coaching and follow-up. It's a powerful tool, but if poorly guided it will require thinking against priorities and perspective due to poor management and coaching. It's a strategic tool with a lack of focus on the business.

- Creating formats without any functionality or required information again shows poor management skills and direction, and lack of ability to define the scope of the tool.

In terms of Home Office, overprocessing is not understanding your customer needs and failing to understand the information at hand, going back and forth with what is thought to be correct without gauging strategic direction. If it's similar to what happens at the physical facility, at least in Mexico, it's having great disregard from top management about what everybody should be doing and accounted for so the business can meet its monthly goals. That said, everybody overprocesses starting from top management because of lack of professionalism.

WAITING (TIME ON HAND)

Workers merely watching an automated machine process material into a finished good, standing around waiting for the next processing step like copying a format in the copy room, looking for an unavailable tool, allowing the coffee machine to heat water and drip coffee into the mug, or simply having work delayed due to stockouts, lot processing delays, equipment downtime, and capacity bottlenecks can all lead to wasted time. These situations break the continuity or flow of processes and cause delays in work-in-progress (WIP).

The challenge is to find a way to complete work according to a standard or avoid distractions that pull your attention away from the task at hand. Waiting is a facilitator of distraction and disrupts the continuity of operation.

Any delay between when one process step ends and the next begins is a waiting time window in which the rhythm is broken or the operator gets distracted and possibly forgets a component, or a machine requires restarting and needs startup setup with material being scrapped.

Some possible reasons for waiting include:

- Waiting for document release, such as a production order on ERP or a process inspection sheet to be signed by the available supervisor or quality engineer, or for the wire transfer to be authorized by the controller. These are reviews or authorizations that halt processes until they happen.

- Waiting for documents at the printer. Formats, reports, or documentation for a case are required for a gate, customer, regulations, audits.

- Standing by an automated machine until it finishes its cycle. Because there was no other activity programmed for the person operating the machine, they stand idle in front of it.

- Standing inside an elevator until the doors open again. Waiting for machine availability to board it and get to the next destination can be similar to waiting for the metro at the station.

- Waiting for raw material to move from warehouse to business unit or be available at workstation to complete work.

- Standing by a computer while it's starting up, loading a document, or compiling a program.

Waiting is associated with idle time while something becomes available to transport, operate, or consolidate, such as making a cup of coffee. These periods can be challenging for people who struggle with being alone, overvalue their time, or stress at the thought of people waiting. We can categorize this "muda" or waste into two types:

- **Unproductive Muda**: This includes waiting times that do not contribute to productivity, do not help build rapport, and might distract from the task at hand. Examples include waiting for a cake to bake in the oven, leaving a customer waiting, or piling up work orders. These waiting times can become distractors and potentially create problems in the business or safety hazards.

- **Productive Muda**: This involves waiting times that can help create bonding and trust. They are productive on a direct level and show the true colors of each individual with humility.

UNNECESSARY TRANSPORT OR CONVEYACE

Transporting work in process (WIP) over long distances can be considered unnecessary. If anything moves more than 45 feet, it can be categorized as unnecessary transport; the 45 feet comes from the distance between columns inside an industrial facility. This creates inefficient transport, or moving materials, parts, or finished goods into or out of storage or between processes.

Unnecessary transport or conveyance is a broad topic. Besides the unofficial 45 feet of distance, consider that anything requiring additional movement of goods (for people it's unnecessary motion) is a form of waste. This could be due to a manufacturing engineer adding an extra foot of conveyor, or the warehouse route being so inefficient that it requires five different individual trips for each good instead of a consolidated trip from the warehouse to the production line.

Let's redefine necessary transport as any smart transportation of materials that can be consolidated and is within the equipment's capabilities. For instance, a 2-ton skid shouldn't be moved by a pallet cart with a 1.5-ton capacity nameplate. Unnecessary transport should not be used to cover up a design mistake or avoid further movement by putting items inside a carton box that might break due to excess weight.

Examples of unnecessary transport include:

- Physically moving a purchase requisition and leaving the individual requisition one per each intention. This could be due to the maximum amount per purchase requisition, the number of signatures required, and the dynamic of the cost centers allowed per purchase requisition.

- Moving WIP long distances between workstations to absorb the difference between imbalanced workstations. This is often due to a defect in the design of operations or underestimating the issue so that it becomes a challenge.

- Collecting signatures for material or tooling reprocessing outside the plant. This often involves moving one-piece batches between people who need to sign the document.

- Moving finished goods from the end of the production line to inspection as an extra step in the process due to a customer requirement or because the process is unreliable in its current state.

- Moving between cash registers to collect excess money, which means that what has been transported long distances is excess cash in the registers.

Interviews can lead to overprocessing and unnecessary transport, not due to the interview itself, but the need to relocate people to facilities outside a 10-mile radius from their homes. This is common, even to the extent of identifying the 60+ minute commute to work. In this case, what is transported is not people, but talent.

Understanding the processes and activities required by the company can provide a fair perspective of logistics, from where resources come from to fill the company's halls and processes with life. This is often overlooked when opening a new production plant. Instead of looking for a great deal on location, there's a huge gap in understanding where you get your people from, not just the raw material or where the finished good can be taken, consolidated, and transported to their distribution center.

The main pitfall of conveyance is that it's designed into the process by necessity or lack of information but is integrated into the process to allow stations to deal with unbalanced times in the process or hypothetical demand increase. This conveyance waste waits to be processed as time passes, but operators wait idle for material or pieces to arrive at the next station.

This waste can be managed by:

1. Reviewing the layout of the process to understand what and where the material stands.

2. Understanding the distance between workstations and the time it takes for material to travel from one station to the next.

3. Reviewing the capacity and weight of material being transported and understanding what equipment can do if conveyance speed can be increased.

4. Reviewing the balance chart of the process, understanding imbalances between stations, and checking if workload can be distributed between stations if allowed by the process.

5. Trying to understand conveyance as material required to fill space between stations.

6. Understanding WIP required based on time material requires to be processed in next station. If process needs balancing, distance should be shortened so travel takes half cycle time.

7. Redesigning layout, minimizing distances between stations and work performed if relocation of electrical, pneumatical, hydraulics, and intranet droppings is required.

Conveyance can be related to diligence mistakes or leaving this understanding to be dealt with in a more advanced stage of implementation process. More importantly:

- Failing to understand amount of material needed at each workstation by either cycle time required for parts to be processed and leave for next operation in process.

- Failing to understand how material can be provided to workstation. This means designing workstation to receive material in quantities required at moment it's needed. Also considering equipment needed to take material to workstation due to volume and weight of material or conditions it must be safely manipulated without injuring personnel.

- Underestimating transport and workstation requirements which may include not understanding requirement. This underestimation is related to implementing generic solution without having studied whole situation or having fix that may be temporary but not permanent.

EXCESS INVENTORY

Excess raw material, work in progress (WIP), or finished goods can lead to longer lead times, obsolescence, damaged goods, transportation and storage costs, and delays. Here are some issues related to excess inventory:

- **Longer Lead Times**: Waiting to accumulate WIP or managing larger batches to move or process into the next step in the process can extend lead times.

- **Obsolescence**: Obsolete items can be hidden among WIP. While a one-piece flow makes it easy to manage obsolescence, it becomes difficult when producing in batches without close control over where components have been assembled.

- **Damaged Goods**: Damaged goods can be hidden among assembled components or in excess inventory. This could be due to the manipulation of finished goods or a component failing tests and being left with good parts.

- **Transportation and Storage Costs**: These are incurred by moving and managing finished goods between the production floor and the warehouse. This includes creating part numbers at given locations in the ERP and dealing with mistakes reported by the ERP due to excess inventory.

Excess inventory also hides problems such as production imbalances, late deliveries from suppliers, defects, equipment downtime, and long setup times. Here are some common characteristics of excess inventory:

- Material procured according to the forecasted demand for the whole year. At some point in the year, there may be a change in customer demand.

- Overproduction of components or finished goods that are now inventory waiting for customer demand.

- Material procured without considering new product introduction programs that may make some components obsolete.

- Materials without a place requiring more work to process as they need to be traced and maintained until given disposition.

- Components used in large conveyance systems requiring more material flooding the system so the next station does not stop due to lack of work.

- Material that answers to a delay in updating information in the planning and follow-up of the production plan.

- Material requiring an additional step to make it functional, like galvanizing the part, deburring, polishing, and tightening bolts and nuts to a required torque value.

If you suspect there's excess inventory, for example, obsolete material, you can follow these steps:

1. Review the material changes, make a list of all the characteristics that have changed and have the latest drawing on hand.

2. Make a list of the part numbers that have been affected by the changes.

3. Add to the part number list the date when the changes were made, so that any lot manufactured before that date is obsolete, anything manufactured after that date is suspicious.

4. Track each lot and inspect every part if possible, to verify that all the materials in that lot are not obsolete.

5. After clearing the warehouse, have a layout of the plant and indicate where the part is integrated into the product and from that point to further up in the process, all the product is suspicious and needs to be checked.

6. If in point 5 there's obsolete material in the finished product, this needs to be discreetly reported as to track the customer's orders produced and affected after the date the new parts were introduced. Identify the production orders and customer's orders that have obsolete components as to reduce the scope.

If there's excess inventory as overproduction:

7. Review the production plan. Check for the total amount of components at the end of each process.

8. Identify the critical components of each part number, as to identify single components that should be in the production area.

9. Have a layout of the production line and identify the process that transforms the material, or the workstations.

10. Have a tour, physically identify each one of the components and count them, then check the totals against what the production plan suggests.

11. Identify discrepancies between quantities declared in production plan against physical inventory, try to trace mistakes to production journals or hourly status boards. Try to identify components that will not be part of production plan because they will be part of excess inventory.

Excess inventory can always be regarded as overproduction and overprocessing because it is work performed while there is no production order that will absorb quantity or work required to deal with inventory.

Avoiding excess inventory should be easy by doing follow-up to production plan, identifying production orders, avoiding any new customer order falling into impossible time frames, having efficient communications on updates on new product introduction programs, and being able to escalate news coming from suppliers when they close their business or need to give maintenance to tooling which creates opportunity to procure more material only to protect customer or being able to deliver.

UNNECESSARY MOVEMENT

Unnecessary motion refers to any wasted movement employees need to perform while they work. However, it's important to note that not all activities that don't directly transform something are a waste. For instance:

- Building rapport while waiting may not directly contribute to KPIs, but it can foster a healthy work environment, improve resilience, and provide a better understanding of business perspectives.

- Looking both ways before crossing the street or aisle may not be part of transforming raw material into finished goods, but it's a great practice for safety and mindfulness.

Activities such as looking for, reaching for, or stacking parts, tools, etc., and even walking can be considered waste. However, in certain environments like a kitchen (unless it's a taco place), cooks need to walk to get ingredients, reach to get a pan, and stack plates when they are washed. This is how their kitchen is designed to meet their requirements and activities.

Unnecessary movements aren't necessarily waste. In a manufacturing operation, eliminating this waste might increase profit margins. But in other businesses and dynamics, these movements are part of the creative process like writing a book or painting a canvas. Even in a home office setting, dealing with minor things at home like maintenance can be part of the work process.

Managers who obsessively see this as an impediment to achieving faster results might consider the following as unnecessary movements:

- Going to the bathroom.

- Fetching the required paperwork, raw material, or tools.

- Eating.

- Fetching a replacement for personal protection equipment like work gloves and safety glasses.

However, it's important to understand that these activities are often necessary for the well-being and productivity of employees.

The term "needless movement of people" is an oversimplification of the concept of MUDA. A more accurate definition would be any movement that does not contribute to preserving the essential workflow, nurturing habits, and creating the discipline and focus required for the task at hand. Any actions that do not align with this spirit should be considered MUDA. However, it's important to acknowledge that addressing physical needs is essential and should be respected as a right. Therefore, unnecessary movements should be categorized as either needful or frivolous.

In the context of kitchen design, unnecessary movement can be a result of poor workstation layout. For instance, if an operator has to walk more than three feet to access their tools and materials, or if they need to twist awkwardly to reach a tool, these are signs of inefficient design.

To minimize unnecessary movements and increase efficiency in a given operation, it's crucial to understand what the operator is doing. This can be achieved by following these steps:

1. **Define the Scope of Analysis**: Limit the study to the specific operation and identify the individuals involved. This helps focus efforts and defines where the study begins and ends.

2. **Understand the Problem***: Identify what, where, how, and when. Be specific ad clear, providing numbers and their origins for transparency. If the metrics are too complex to explain, they may not be suitable for tracking progress.

3. **Understand the Operation**: Provide a brief description of the tasks, the cycle time of the workstation, the planned cycle time, the takt time, and the tools required.

4. **Observe the Operation**: In addition to point three, observe the operation firsthand. Understand each step, noting any deviations such as a tool being used that isn't mentioned in the standard procedure.

5. **Create a Layout of the Operation**: Update as needed to reflect the actual distribution. Use this spaghetti diagram to indicate if the operator moves to retrieve raw materials or tools. Measure the distances that the operator must travel to complete their work.

6. **Gather Information**: Compile data on workstation distances and deviations found in standard work. Understand both the declared cycle time of the station and the actual cycle time based on findings.

7. **Review Tools**: Understand if overprocessing occurs because current tools lack capacity or if tooling is

required to ensure assembly according to specification.

8. **Review Distances**: Understand if travel distances can be reduced by having raw materials within 3 feet of operation or designing a material delivery rack. Also, consider whether tools can be dedicated to a workstation or if they contribute to overprocessing.

9. **Update Standard Work Sheets**: Document real operations and train personnel on new processes based on remediations from operation analysis.

Movements can be minimized by implementing the following strategies:

• **Design and Analyze the Operation**: Ensure that the operator has the necessary tools and tooling.

• **Check Tool Capacity**: Compare the tool's capacity with the product's specifications and validate the tool's capability with a gauge R&R.

• **Deliver Materials to Workstation**: Arrange for materials to be delivered directly to the workstation.

• **Design an Efficient Workstation**: Incorporate poka-yokes and integrated tooling into the workstation design to prevent mistakes and reduce overprocessing.

• **Update Standard Work Documentation**: Keep standard work documentation up-to-date with the latest operation to avoid any deviation in the operation.

DEFECTS

Defects, which are deviations from a specification, an ideal physical form, a boundary sample, or a performance test, can occur during operation or fabrication, at the end of the line, or even among items in warehouse stock. To prevent and detect defects, consider the following:

- **Train Personnel**: Use a standard operation worksheet that outlines each step of the process, including which tools to use, where to source raw materials and tools, and how to place materials on the tooling.

- **Design and Specify Equipment**: Ensure equipment can restart operations after an electricity or emergency shutdown. Stations should track operations programmed in their PLC and only start operations when a part is present or restart the sequence when the piece is removed from the tooling.

- **Review Drawings for New Products**: Collaborate with engineering to consider poke yokes from the part design and how they can be integrated into workstation tooling.

- **Implement a Manufacturing Execution System (MES)**: This requires documentation of standard operations, trained personnel, specified and implemented equipment and devices to detect components and movements, poke yokes installed into the process and tooling to ensure correct installation of raw material into machines, and verification of materials recorded on the ERP.

Implementing these measures can prevent defects from progressing into finished products or reaching customers. It also prevents defects from being further processed, which would consume resources and create more waste. Defects can lead to:

- **Overprocessing**: A defect may require additional processing to achieve desired performance or assembly.

- **Overproduction**: If defects are not addressed, further production may occur just to meet production order or customer request quantities.

- **Waste of Conveyance**: Defects can lead to unnecessary raw material movement as people attempt to process the defect.

- **Waste of Inventory****: Defects hidden among materials that need maintenance can lead to waste.

- **Waiting**: Disposal of defective material may cause operators to wait idle for decisions to be made.

HOME OFFICE

While a home office is not inherently flawed, it can present challenges if not properly designed. In a traditional office setting, services such as cleaning, supply replenishment, and maintenance are typically provided. However, when work is transferred to the home, these services often fall on the individual, sometimes even at a reduced wage. This can lead to a poorly designed workspace and potential mishaps, such as a makeshift laptop stand collapsing and damaging the laptop.

This lack of design can result in additional costs, such as replacing damaged equipment or traveling to the nearest office store to purchase a new laptop. These costs can be deducted from the paycheck, adding administrative and transportation costs.

Compared to a traditional office or manufacturing shop floor, a home office is uncharted territory. It's often seen as just a place to relax on the couch in the living room, rather than a space for productive work. Therefore, it's crucial to properly design and equip your home office to ensure it's conducive for work.

Here are some basic rules for maintaining a productive home office:

1. **Stay Active**: Even without a dedicated home office, avoid lounging on the couch. Maintain good grooming habits, stay in shape for physical activities, and continue to hone skills that improve your reaction time to daily challenges. Engage in hobbies that keep you active and attentive.

2. **Understand Different Situations**: Not all situations require action or correction. The most important skill is to listen and understand the situation without jumping to conclusions. Hobbies can help you develop rapport with those closest to you. Remember, if you struggle with rapport at work, it's likely the same in your personal life.

3. **Maintain a Clean and Healthy Image**: Adopt habits like reading for at least 30 minutes daily, scheduling regular physical workouts, and maintaining personal hygiene. These habits will keep you, your most important asset, available for work.

4. **Designate a Workspace**: Have a space for work that can be separated from the rest of the house. You can't have a meeting with background noise like dogs barking or someone yelling at the gardener. It's not about isolating yourself from your home, but rather about having a dedicated time and space for work.

5. **Don't Accept Pay Cuts for Working from Home**: It's great if you can make working from home work for you, but don't accept a pay cut in exchange for this convenience. Always understand the need to keep time and space separate for work and family.

6. **Budget for Home Office Expenses**: Your home office will increase usage of utilities like internet, water, electricity, gas, and cleaning

supplies. Sometimes it may be necessary to have a separate internet service or a room separated from the rest of your house.

7. **Maintain a Schedule**: Keep a schedule not just for work hours, but also for cleaning, checking emails, dealing with critical items of the day, preparing lunch, and handling home issues that could affect your work performance.

Remote work, while not a defect, can present challenges if not properly managed. In a traditional office, services like cleaning and supply replenishment are provided. However, when work shifts to the home, these responsibilities often fall on the individual. This can lead to a poorly designed workspace and potential mishaps.

To succeed in remote work, consider the following:

1. **Set Clear Expectations**: Understand your responsibilities and expectations before starting remote work.

2. **Communicate Regularly**: Regular communication with your team members and manager is crucial.

3. **Stay Organized**: Use project management tools and calendars to keep track of your tasks and deadlines.

4. **Set Boundaries**: Create a clear distinction between your work and personal life.

5. **Leverage Flexibility**: Use the flexibility of remote work to your advantage by working during your most productive hours.

If you're seeking alternatives to remote work, consider jobs that offer a mix of office and home-based work or flexible roles like contract or freelance positions.

Here are some additional tips for remote work:

6. **Create a Dedicated Workspace**: This helps you stay focused and productive.

7. **Take Breaks**: Regular breaks can help maintain your productivity levels.

8. **Stay Connected**: Regular check-ins with your team can foster a sense of community.

9. **Self-Care**: Prioritize your physical and mental health by maintaining a healthy lifestyle.

By following these tips, you can enhance your remote work experience and performance.

Working from home, while increasingly popular, can present unique challenges. However, with the right strategies, you can stay productive and focused. Here are some tips for optimizing your home office experience:

1. **Establish a Dedicated Workspace**: Choose a quiet, well-lit space in your home equipped with essentials like a desk, chair, computer, and office supplies. This helps separate your work life from your personal life.

2. **Create a Routine**: Set specific times for starting and ending your workday, and take regular breaks. This helps you stay on track and maintain productivity.

3. **Take Regular Breaks**: Stand up and move around every 20-30 minutes to avoid restlessness or

fatigue. Step outside for fresh air or do some light exercises.

4. **Minimize Distractions**: Work in a quiet space where you won't be interrupted. Turn off your phone and close any unnecessary tabs on your computer.

5. **Dress for Work**: Dressing up for work, even at home, helps maintain a productive mindset.

6. **Practice Self-Care**: Ensure you get enough sleep, eat healthy foods, and exercise regularly. This helps keep you energized and focused.

7. **Stay Connected**: Regularly connect with colleagues and friends to combat feelings of isolation. This could involve setting up video calls or sending emails or text messages.

Additional tips include:

- Use time tracking software to monitor productivity.

- Set daily and weekly goals.

- Leverage online resources and tools like project management software and cloud storage.

- Seek feedback from colleagues and supervisors to improve productivity.

Working from home offers numerous benefits, including improved work-life balance and increased productivity. However, it's also important to be gentle with yourself during this process. Here are some tips:

8. **Set Realistic Expectations**: Don't expect to match office productivity levels immediately. It's okay to take breaks, run errands, or attend to personal matters. The key is to return to work promptly.

9. **Avoid Comparisons**: Everyone has a unique work pace and style. Avoid comparing yourself to others and focus on your own progress.

10. **Be Kind to Yourself**: Mistakes are part of the learning process, especially when transitioning to remote work. Learn from them and move forward without self-criticism.

11. **Prioritize Self-Care**: Ensure you get enough sleep, eat healthily, and exercise regularly. Your physical and mental health directly impact your productivity.

12. **Ask for Help**: Don't hesitate to seek help from colleagues, supervisors, or loved ones when needed. They can provide support and advice when you're feeling overwhelmed.

Additional tips include:

- Allocate Personal Time: Set aside time each day for relaxation and rejuvenation activities like walking, reading, or spending time with loved ones.

- Take Regular Breaks: Stand up and move around every 20-30 minutes to avoid restlessness or fatigue.

- Create a Comfortable Workspace: Ensure your workspace is well-lit, organized, and equipped with everything you need.

- Maintain Mental Health: Stay connected with others as remote work can be isolating. Reach out to friends and family, join virtual communities, or seek professional help if needed.

By following these tips, you can create a positive work-from-home experience while being gentle with yourself.

Having a dedicated workspace in your home office is crucial for several reasons. Firstly, it can enhance focus and productivity by providing a specific place for work, thereby minimizing distractions. Secondly, it can promote a better work-life balance by creating a physical separation between your work and personal space. Lastly, it can boost organization and efficiency by having everything you need within reach.

Here are some tips for setting up a dedicated workspace in your home office:

1. **Choose a Quiet Space**: Find a place that is quiet and free from distractions. This could be a spare bedroom, a corner of your living room, or even a closet.

2. **Ensure Good Lighting**: Good lighting is essential for productivity. Ensure the space is well-lit, either naturally or artificially.

3. **Invest in Comfortable Furniture**: Comfort is key as you'll be spending a lot of time in your workspace. Invest in a good desk, chair, and other necessary accessories.

4. **Personalize Your Space**: Add personal touches to make the space feel like your own. This could

include pictures, plants, or other items that you enjoy.

5. **Keep Your Workspace Organized**: An organized workspace promotes productivity. Keep your workspace tidy and free of clutter.

6. **Take Breaks**: Regular breaks are important to avoid restlessness or fatigue. Stand up and move around every 20-30 minutes.

7. **Set Boundaries**: Establish clear boundaries between work and personal life. Avoid checking work emails or messages outside of work hours.

Additional tips include:

- **Ensure Proper Ventilation**: A well-ventilated workspace helps keep you alert and focused.

- **Use Noise-Cancelling Headphones**: These can help block out distractions.

- **Create a Daily To-Do List**: Prioritize your tasks to stay on track and avoid feeling overwhelmed.

- **End Your Workday Positively**: This helps you feel refreshed and ready for the next day.

By following these tips, you can create a comfortable, productive, and organized workspace in your home office.

Good lighting is crucial for a productive home office. It enhances visibility, prevents eye strain, and promotes alertness. There are two primary types of lighting to consider: natural light and artificial light.

- **Natural Light**: This is the best type of light for your home office. It's bright, even, and helps regulate your circadian rhythm. If possible, choose a workspace with plenty of natural light. If your workspace lacks natural light, supplement it with artificial light.

- **Artificial Light**: There are various types of artificial light available. Choose the right type based on your needs. For general tasks like writing or reading, opt for a bright, diffused light source. For more detailed tasks like photo or video editing, a more focused light source is needed.

Here are some tips for creating a well-lit home office:

1. **Combine Natural and Artificial Light**: This provides the best lighting conditions.

2. **Place Your Desk Near a Window**: This allows you to utilize natural light.

3. **Use Task Lighting**: This provides focused light for specific tasks.

4. **Install Dimmer Switches**: These allow you to adjust the light intensity as needed.

5. **Avoid Fluorescent Lighting**: This type of lighting can be harsh and cause eye strain.

6. **Maintain a Clean Workspace**: A clutter-free workspace maximizes light.

Additional tips include:

- **Use Light-Colored Walls and Furniture**: These reflect light and make your workspace feel brighter.

- **Add Plants**: Plants improve air quality and help diffuse light.

- **Clean Your Windows Regularly**: This allows more natural light to enter.

- **Use Blinds or Curtains**: These control the amount of natural light in your workspace.

By following these tips, you can create a comfortable, productive, and well-lit home office.

NOTES

NOTES

NOTES

NOTES

NOTES

NOTES